Out of Chaos

Poetry and Prayer

By Carol Ingram

beardsANDbicycles

ISBN-10 0615922945

This book is dedicated to my Dad.
Willie George Salter
September 14, 1931 – February 20, 2013

Contents

Part 3.......The Journey

Part 1

From Dust

So much beauty fashioned from dust

Dust

When you kneeled before them,

water basin and towel in hand
washing the dust from their feet,
did you remember?

Did you think of the beginning,
when you took dust;
dust of the Earth
and formed them?

Did you kneel then too;
with water
creating them in your image?

Did you realize, as you dusted off
your new creation,
that one day you would kneel again
at their feet
in service to them
reclaiming them for your kingdom?

O, what Love...

Sand, Water and Sky

Sun awakens my body
nourishing warmth, energy.

Gentle tides slow my rhythm,
balancing it once again with yours.

Quietly I walk, noticing,
collecting your gifts.

Gifts from your depths;
shells, starfish, sand dollars.

Sun fades, stars shine,
warm winds embrace me.

I feel your presence,
know your love.

In this holy place
of sand, water and sky.

Receive the Gift

It came
wrapped in starlight and mystery
wrapped eons ago.
Wrappings gently unfolded over thirty some years,
unveiling the mystery hidden in centuries of revelation.

We had vague glimpses
words of love, acts of kindness, gentleness...
deep joy...laughter...
the wine at the wedding, the healings...such compassion
we had seen the veil almost lifted that day on the mountain
standing with them on such holy ground.

Everything changed...
the journey to Jerusalem...the palms of joy...
the reality of rejection...
that heartbreaking night in the garden...
the cross...the stone covered tomb.

Then the unveiled Glory of our Lord!

And now, now the gift is loose,
wind and fire, flowing freely, radiantly
to all who choose to receive it.
Choose, dear one, receive the gift.
It really is for you!

Awakening

A soft, tender movement
A fresh breath
Fragrant
Vibrant
Pregnant with possibility

It's sacred
A bit unknown

It's Spirit
Stirring the chaos
Shifting the waters
Whispering
Breathing

It's life
Groaning, struggling, singing

It's transforming
Growing with pains
Expanding
Giving birth
Uniting us as one.

Nourishment

It came with intensity,
In the heat of the moment.
Thunder rumbling
Dark clouds blocking the sun,
Foreboding in the air.

Cats hiding in the barn
Buster curled up on the porch
The birds quiet down.
Waiting in some hidden place
They all know it's coming.

Thunder breaks open the quiet.
Lightning awakens nature's awareness.
Dark clouds burst open.
Rain pelts the earth.

The air permeated with fragrance
Is more than wet.
It smells of earth, trees, farm, animals,
Musty and moist.

The elemental earth has no choice,
It must accept this powerful deluge.
The trees cannot run and hide
The grass has nothing to curl up under
The elements must accept what they are experiencing.

Proud trees receive the nourishing rain,
Bending to the cool calming winds.

Intensity increases.
Lightning strikes a proud tree.
It bravely takes the pruning,
Branches falling to the ground.

Earth is saturated.
This nourishment is more than it can bear.
Moisture puddles up.
More can be absorbed...later.

Thunder now rumbles in the distance.
The rain subsides.
Leaves glisten with pearls of nourishment,
Pearls that dance gracefully along the limbs
Down the slick green sides of the pears
Hanging heavily on plump figs.

Wind orchestrates movements,
Blowing heavy clouds away.
Rainbow colors blue sky.
Puddles evaporate,
Pruned limbs die.
Fruits grow.
Nourished.

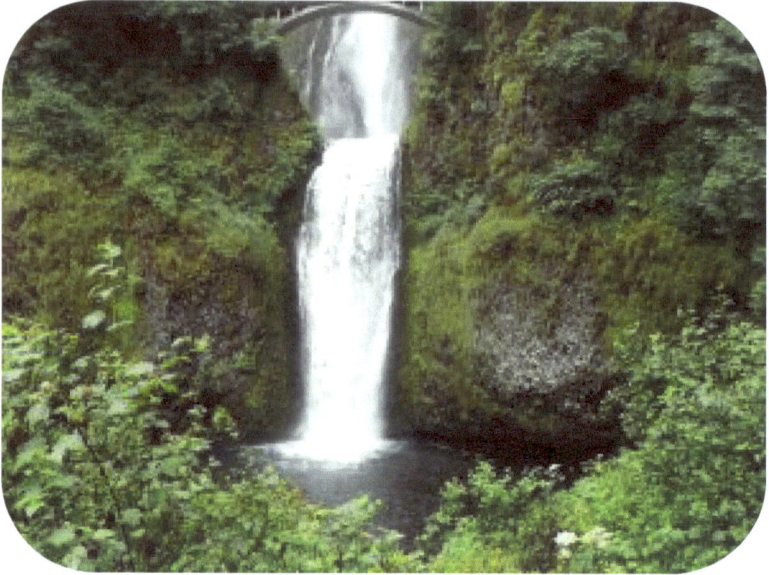

SSSHHH!!!

The waterfall spoke to me.
Its loud rushing waves yelled.

SSSSSSHHHHHH!

Inviting me to be quiet
Be still
Listen
See
Notice
The beauty
The majesty
The creation
That is.

Second Chances

I hear them again this morning.
A symphony of sorts,
Coming from the trees.
The dappling sunlight
Reflects a row of translucent brown bumps.
A vertical parade of cicada shells
Precariously hanging from bark, twigs, leaves.

Gapping scars bear witness
To transformation, the physical struggle.
A tearing away of the old self
A freeing of the new, inner life.

Yes, it is a symphony!
Rejoicing at the gift of second chances.

Caves

What's inside the darkness?
      Is it just a shelter?
          A passageway?
              Perhaps a hiding place?
                  Is there a secret stored inside?
I need to explore.
Find my way...

It's quiet inside
      Inspiring me to rest, reflect.
          It feels like a cathedral.
             A sacred place;
                Is that what draws me?
That sense of the sacred?

Perhaps God holds some things in darkness.
      As mystery;
          So we seekers will come,
             Explore
And find the sacred in the mystery.

Blackbirds

Dancing outside my window again today.
Showing off their precision.
Hundreds, moving as one
These ordinary black birds
Become a magnificent display
Of harmony
Of community
Of oneness.

And I long for humanity to dance like these ordinary black
birds.

Broken

What if brokenness is the beginning

Of transformation?

What if our need is not to fix our brokenness,

But to allow it to transform us?

An egg is cracked,
Broken by the new life emerging.
So it is with a cocoon.
A mother's water breaks
Birthing the new life inside her.

Perhaps when the Divine Spirit
Breaks through in our hearts
New life emerges in us.

We are reborn
Transformed by brokenness.

Part 2

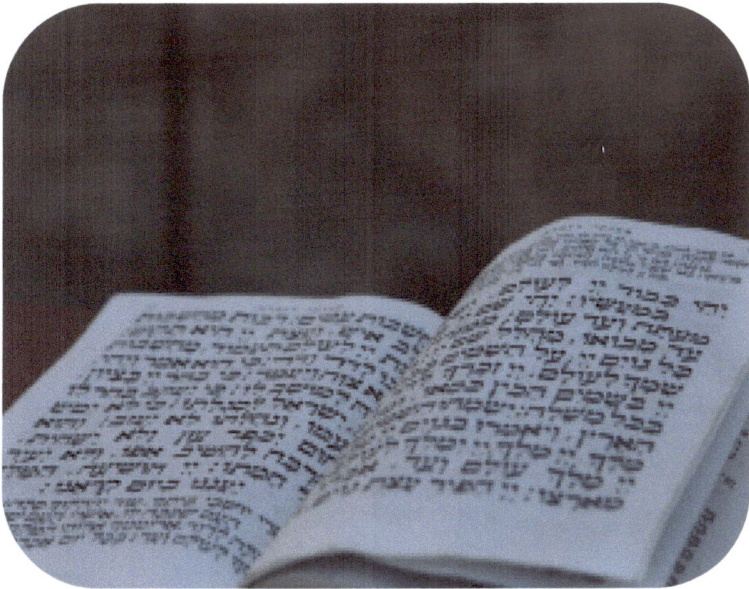

To Words

Balanced by words of love

The Word of God

Enticing words

Mystery and truth

Poetry and prose

Historical fiction and non-fiction

God-breathed and hand-written

Metaphorical and literal

Useful and used

Powerful and provocative

Read and rejected

Studied and preached

Timeless and eternal

These words bind us to Love

And release us to freedom.

Oh!

Oh, love me, right now and hold me; just the way you promised.
Oh, love me, right now and hold me; just the way you.
Oh, love me, right now and hold me; just the way.
Oh, love me, right now and hold me; just.
Oh, love me, right now and hold me.
Oh, love me, right now.
Oh, love me right.
Oh, love me.
Oh, love.
Oh!

Adapted from Psalm 119:76

The Lord

My Shepherd
Provider
Restorer
Guide

I face shadows
Unafraid.

Your Presence
Comforts me.

Abundance
Joy
Goodness
Love

All companions
On my journey home.

Based on Psalm 23

Forgiveness

Is it really about a number, seventy times seven?
Four-hundred ninety times I forgive you, and then it's over.

Is it about repentance?
If you turn away from your sin then I will forgive you.

Is it about healing?
When I feel healed from the damage your sin inflicted on me I
will forgive you.

Is forgiveness a choice?
When I am ready I will choose to forgive you.

Or is it an act of the Spirit?
Something I cannot control.
Something that happens within me
As I make myself at home in Your Love.

One of Those Days

Ever had one of those days?
The kind that starts with unexpected, difficult news.
News that sends your emotions bouncing around your heart
Leaving tender raw places.
You just want to be alone.
Cry it out.

But you can't manage that,
Not at the moment
Life has demands.
The work load is heavy,
Feels burdensome.
Yet the need is great.

And so you stay and work
Until all the needs are met.

Then, at the end of this long tiring day,
As people are leaving, heading home,
You sigh.
Finally alone,
You seek solace in prayer
Pouring out your needs late into the evening.

You emerge; refreshed, renewed, and energized
Walking on water into a new day.

Inspired by Matthew 14

Stones Fall

Naked

Accusations

Truth

Jesus

Trembling

Alone

Before Jesus

No condemnation

Based on John 8:1-11

Judas

Imagine if you will
Going to your church,
Confessing a sin—a betrayal,
Only to find out
They don't care;
They turn you away.

Distraught and desperate
You take your own life.

Imagine if you will
On the other side of this life
You find a High Priest
That does care,
That welcomes you,
Forgives you,
Loves you.

And knows your name is Judas.

Mary

Perhaps, she listened
with the ears of her heart,
understood what was coming,
poured out her best gift
on Jesus
anointing Him for burial.

Perhaps, the others
angry, indignant,
hadn't truly heard,
until He said,
"No more, let her alone."

Based on Mark 14:3-9

Invitation

A dinner invitation
Issued by Matthew
Everyone invited
Disciples, religious scholars,
Pharisees and disreputable characters.

A banquet invitation
Issued by God
Everyone invited
Sick, dirty, starving, poor
Backstabbers, broken.

Will you join them at the table?

Let It Be

That day the angel came
Offering news of a baby,
God's son being born.
You said, "Let it be."

As you faced the possible stoning
The looks, the taunts
Over the untimely pregnancy.
Did you say, "Let it be?"

When your water broke
Your baby coming
At the end of a long journey
When offered the humble stable,
Did you say, "Let it be?"

As you watched your son heal so many people
So soon after your own husband had died.
Did you ever wonder why your son
Did not heal your husband?
Or did you say, "Let it be?"

That dark day
When you stood at the foot of your son's cross
Received his instruction to take John as your new son.
Did you say, "Let it be?"

On the third day when you heard the news,
Resurrection news.
Could you believe?
God had let this be.

A Morning Prayer

Loving God,
I shout Hallelujahs to your name this morning,
as I seek you in prayer.

I ask that you help me to be true today;
true to myself and to others.

Help me to love my enemies
to allow them to bring out the best in me,
not the worst.

When someone gives me a hard time today,
give me the energy to pray for them.

Give me a heart of generosity,
expressed in actions.

I truly desire to live out this God-created identity you have
given me, help me to express kindness to all,
as you are kind to me, even when I am at my worst.

Create in me the desire to be easy on people.

Give me a discerning heart as I choose my teachers.

Teach me to take your words of truth
and work them into my life as a foundation;
may they be words on which I build my life.

And may all of these requests honor you and your Kingdom
work. Amen.

Prayer inspired by Luke 6:28-49

A Simple Psalm

O Lord, I am a simple woman
From a farming community,
A nomad on this journey,
Not a theologian.

My soul has found rest in you in many quiet places;
The sands of the Gulf
The hills of Tennessee
The lush Galilee
The cathedrals of Europe
The journey of the labyrinth
The soil of the Earth
And the "SSSHHH" of the waterfall.

O nations and peoples of the Earth,
Let us put our hope in the Lord
The time of renewal is here.

Inspired by Psalm 131

Part 3

The Journey

Into silence and light

I Need to Know That You Love Me

When you see me on the street today
in rumpled clothes, crying
Know that God loves me.

If I am rushing by in a suit
ignoring you, on my way to important people
Know that God loves me.

If I appear angry with my kids in tow
rattled by their incessant words
Know that God loves me.

If I have clothes on that make you uncomfortable
and my skin is different from yours
Know that God loves me.

If I appear to be under the influence of drugs or alcohol
yearning for another fix
Know that God loves me.

If I tell you I am hungry or homeless
do not be afraid of me
Know that God loves me.

Whoever I am and however I seem to you...
Don't walk away from me
for I Am
and I need to know that you love me.

Coventry

Sitting on that bench
In the midst of a scarred shell
Brick walls blackened by fire
Statues charred and broken
Trying to grasp what happened here.

Inside the blackened shell, an altar of forgiveness,
A cross above, fashioned from the ruins,
Erected to remind nations and peoples of God's forgiveness:
Forgiveness for acts of war,
Forgiveness for the pain humankind pours out on one
another.

My eyes move to a monument of reconciliation.
A man and a woman
On their knees,
       Embracing,
           Weeping,
               Humble,
                   Forgiving,
                       Loving.

Just beyond, the path to a newly built cathedral
Radiant with God's glory
A window of radiant colors: sapphires, emeralds, rubies
Surrounding the glorious amber light filled center.

The light of a bomb left behind the first scarred shell.
The light of God's glory radiates the second.
Darkness and destruction overcome by Light.

Sitting within the scarred ruins
Saddened by the pain felt here
Encouraged by the hope of renewal
Fascinated by those who had the courage to rebuild.

Shedding

The tree trunk
stands silent in the forest
bark slowly breaking away
revealing a smooth core of solid wood.

With the protective covering now shed
I see the beauty of the wood
the circles of stories
standing in the forest
waiting for someone to listen.

Acceptance

I take his hand
No one notices the pressure he puts on mine
We're just father and daughter walking.

They don't notice that I'm driving now.
Expected to know the way
Digesting the test results
Asking the questions
Offering explanations
Wondering if he understands
Trusted to make decisions.

I watch him come out of the local grocery store.
He found the bread
He can't find the right car
I watch and wait
I'm just one car over
He sees me and comes
Heartbroken, I say nothing.

The shift so subtle
I never saw it coming
But he did.

"Dad, do you think you are getting Alzheimer's?"
"I believe I am."
"What kind of things are you forgetting?"
"I can't tell you what the doctor said yesterday."
"So what thoughts go through your mind?"
"Sometimes I think about when I was in the army.
There might be a flash of playing with you kids.
Sometimes I will remember something from work."

At home the walls filled with family pictures.
Some just taped there
He admits he's trying to keep the names and faces together.

Is it easy some days?
Lost on others?
I don't ask.

He seems so child-like, Lord
What does it look like to honor my father in this season of
life?

Acceptance
Presence
Prayer
Offered in love
Clothed with humility and respect.

I have to go home today
Seven hundred miles away
Will he remember me when I come back
Or will I be the face he has lost?

Strength to carry my baggage to the car
Hugs and kisses
Tears he doesn't see as I drive away
My stomach in knots.

This does not feel like acceptance!

"Beloved daughter
Remember he is mine
I will love him through this season
Trust me."

Trust made acceptance possible.

Sacred Spaces

Big brown eyes
Peeping out the window
Two shadows in the darkness
Gliding back and forth in the swing
Ending a date
That would lead to a marriage.

My turn with a beau in the swing
Cooling off on a hot summer day
His shirt opens to firm tan muscles
We talk and laugh as Hound Dog jumps up to join us
Love is in the air.

My own dreamy nights
Lying in the swing, alone
Star gazing
Filled with wonder
At the universe
At God.

Our long talk about the future:
College? Marriage?
We agree to a lifetime together
I run inside to tell Dad.

Brothers and sisters
Aunts and uncles
Grandkids and cousins
Talking, laughing, sharing life
In and around the swing.

My brother and I discuss the future now:
The bumps in marriage
The cancer that is ravaging his wife's body
The sadness
A new appreciation of life.

Pop swings by himself a lot
He tells me it's a place of prayer
It's also the place he waits:
For us to return
For his beloved family to be reunited.

It's been blown away by hurricanes:
Rebuilt by family
Repainted and roofed in
Only to be blown down again.

And still it stands
As a vessel to hold our most treasured times.

Words of love, promises, laughter, honesty,
Prayer, trust, vulnerability and pain.
It is our family's sacred space.
The place we allow ourselves to love one another,
And be loved by one another.

The old swing in the backyard.

I'd Rather be Busy

Lord, could you put me
to work today?
I need to be busy
Till these feelings go away.

I'd rather be busy.
Keep these feelings at bay
Till they're not so intense
Another time...another day.

So put me to work
Just for today.
I'd rather be busy
Than feel this way.

This grief of mine
It goes so deep.
Tears flowing freely
How can this be?

I want to be peaceful
And happy.
At ease

So keep me busy, Lord
I'd rather be busy
Out there serving you...please.

"Okay, Dear One
I have a job for you."

Yes, Lord, I'm listening
What can I do?

"I have a daughter
Who's crying right now,
Could you be with her,
Somehow?"

O yes, Lord
Let me just wipe off my face.
Who is she Lord?
Will I know her face?

"Yes, Dear one
The daughter is you.
I need you to be
A soul friend to you.
Your grief is important.
Your tears are true,
Let them all flow
That's the work you must do."

But Lord, I'd rather be busy...

Glory

My dear Glory,
You think you chose me
With that big paw grabbing at my hair;
But I'm the one who chose you,
Rescued you from bondage
Paid the ransom price
You are family now.

I woo you with security, food, shelter, water, freedom.
Everything you need
Yet, you hold back from me,
Skittering here and there
Teasing me with your trust.

I desire to hold you, pet you.
You circle in my lap, settle, then in the middle of a sweet purr
Suddenly you pounce away.

I can tell you want to love me, trust me.
As I'm dosing off each night you come to my side.
Watching me, licking my hand, my arm, my face
Close, but on your terms only.

Such insecurity
Is there pain in closeness for you
Perhaps a relationship you had before you came to me
Or just not quite sure of my love yet?

I will give you the time you need to trust.
Wait until you are ready to receive the love.

So much joy in watching you
Running here and there
Scampering up a tree
Chasing everything that moves
Birds, bugs, leaves, the wind

So free and in that freedom
Just perhaps a bit too curious.

I go out to call your name tonight.
You've been out chasing fireflies;
I can't find you.
My heart is heavy.
I desire to have you with me;
Assure you that I love you,
That you are a part of our family.

I start walking
Searching
Calling your name
Sensing you are lost but not gone.

You hear my voice and follow me home
Creeping home beside me in the shadows
But you're not ready to come to me even now
I am teased once more.

Or am I being tested?
I sit outside and wait
Calling once again
Until finally you choose to come bounding into my arms.

Willing to come to me
Accepting that you belong
Ready to abide in my love.

Invitation to Play

Come with me.

We'll swing, hop and skip

Our way to a wonderland.

We'll be superheroes

Or rabbits or maybe a rainbow.

We'll fly, swing and slide

Through our playground.

We'll ride colorful creatures

While music plays.

We'll run with excitement

Into each new adventure.

Awaiting the rush play brings

Oh, the joy in such wide-eyed wonder.

Pathways

Loving God,
I praise you for pathways:

pathways that others walked before me
pathways where light outshines darkness
pathways cleared of debris
pathways that are straight
pathways that I can run, dance and stroll on

Thank you for all the ways, my pathway was made ready for me.

Fears and Choices

Some old fears visited me this morning.
Popped in right out of the blue
Made my heart flutter and flip
Doubts came too...

I panicked at first.
Then reached out to a friend
Sought reassurance and love
My strength came again.

Empowered, I let those fears fall away one by one.

I chose life today,
Over fears.

I chose truth today,
Over lies.

I chose to listen to the voice of love today,
Instead of old doubts.

The victory came with the choice.

Family Reunion

Their names were Sam and Ruth.
Just two people in love
Married, raising a family
Walking with God.

Years later, their descendants gather.
We don't all know one another.
On the street we would just be a familiar face passing by--
But, we are family.

How did we come to live such separate lives?
How is it that we feel unrelated?
Is it time apart?
The space between us...
Or did we just stop reaching out to each other
Did we move on from our sense of family?

If only our world could regain a sense of family.
All humanity related.
And have a big family reunion
Where we reduce the spaces between us:
Reach out with open hands to receive
Those that no longer look familiar
Or think as we do.

Lord, teach our hearts to love
And accept one another as family.

Spin

It happened again this week:
that subtle inner movement
where I spin the words of my narrative
so that all my motivations
all my reasons
look good.

This time I noticed that movement:
caught what I was doing
found the courage to name the things I was spinning
then, as I spoke
I included as much of my truth as I was aware of and found...

Understanding
Love
Acceptance
I found no need to spin.

Dance of the Butterflies

Drawn to this way of prayer
I step onto the labyrinth,
Praying, releasing my burdens
Opening myself to God at each turn.

Nearby, I notice the butterflies
Floating, dancing on the breeze.
I stop to watch, to listen...

Their dance speaks to me of lightness and freedom.
I sit with that image in the middle of the circle,
God's heart...
Allow it to transform my spirit.

I feel the lightness, the freedom
that we have with God
And join the dance of the butterflies.

Is it True?

Like the water flowing through the creek,
The wind blowing through the trees,
Your Spirit moves through my body.

Or...

Is it true...

That the creek embodies the water flowing through it,
The trees give movement to the wind,
And my body is the place
You live and move and have Your being?

Somehow

Somehow, in my spirit, I feel it:

Your presence in the midst of my pain

Your steadfastness where my sorrow rests

Your love holding my loss

And I am in awe of your ways.

How is it that you can be so tender to me

So attentive to my loss?

I beg you, Loving God

Do this for everyone.

What Is It Like For You, Daddy?

Trapped in a body that is shutting down
Moving in and out of awareness
As the morphine deadens the pain.

Will you know it's me when you hear my voice?
Do you want to move on?
Can you?

What are your dreams like?
Can you see heaven?
Is Jesus calling you, comforting you?

Do you feel the pain?
Do you notice as something else shuts down?

Are you remembering the love we have for you?
I sure hope so...

What is it like for you, Daddy?

Unfolding

The Moments

I

Words are not on the tip of my tongue
Not even stuck in my throat,
They are hidden inside
Some place deep.

What I do know is that I am here for the moments.

The moments Dad responds to my voice,
That he reaches up for a hug
Or kisses me back.

The handshake he offered an old friend.
Those times when he reaches out
Touching something unseen in the air.

The moments my tears come
The seconds between his breaths
That I count while holding my breath.

These are the words
I can share from this hidden place
The words I know are true.
I sit vigil for these moments.

II

The moments are gone now.

Faded in that last wisp of breath
That last faint beat of his heart.

I feel the void
An un-fillable longing
An empty place
A Dad-sized hole in my heart.

This movement from moments to memories
Is a salty tear-streaked journey.

Wrenching at times
Soft and gentle at others.

As natural as snow melt
Finding its way to the sea
By way of gentle brooks,
Rapid waterfalls,
Converging rivers.

But it also resembles a hot, humid, thunder storm
Rattling the windows of my broken heart.

The Mystery

The geese remind me
how easy it is
to move
      from land
            to water
                  to sky.

O, the mystery of their ways
as they emerge on a distant shore.

Your Guardian

May you feel the presence of your Guardian God this day.
May your strength come from the knowledge that God is right
at your side;
Ready to protect you.
If you need to leave a situation,
God is your guard.
If you need to return,
God is your guard.
God guards you always, everywhere.
May you have the awareness of this Guardian Presence
Shielding you and sheltering you
In the storms of this life
And in the most ordinary moments of your day.

Into Quiet

A quiet afternoon

on the edge of water and woods.

I hear the leaf break away,

watch it silently float to the ground,

hear the soft crunch as it lands,

the swishing of wind stirring the grasses,

the echoing twitter of a distant bird,

and the still small voice of the Divine.

www.ingramcontent.com/pod-product-compliance
Lightning Source LLC
LaVergne TN
LVHW010029070426
835511LV00004B/98